SHIMMY SHIMMY
COKE-CA-POP!

SHIMMY SHIMMY COKE-CA-POP!

A COLLECTION OF CITY CHILDREN'S STREET GAMES AND RHYMES

BY

JOHN LANGSTAFF AND CAROL LANGSTAFF

PHOTOGRAPHS BY DON MAC SORLEY

DOUBLEDAY & COMPANY, INC.
GARDEN CITY, NEW YORK

To Kate and Meg
who taught us some of these games,
and to little Sarah
who will play many of them as she grows up.

ISBN: 0-385-05769-5 Trade
ISBN: 0-385-05771-7 Prebound
Library of Congress Catalog Card Number 72-92227

Printed in the United States of America

9 8 7 6 5 4 3

Book design and handwriting by M. F. Gazze

CONTENTS

INTRODUCTION

Young children at play in the street, involved with one another and not being directed by adults, seem to have a world of their own. They communicate and interact freely—often by means of a living, oral tradition that has been passed along since ancient times. By nature, children have the ability to move or dance, sing and pantomime; and the chants and rhymes they learn from slightly older children form the basis for these special childhood activities.

It fascinated us to observe this phenomenon of oral tradition so naturally at work on the street. So we set out with a small tape recorder and a camera to see what we could find in various streets, playgrounds, and housing projects in ethnic neighborhoods in Boston, Roxbury, Cambridge, and New York, during the fall, spring, and winter months when children were outdoors after school. The groups we visited included Irish, Puerto Rican, Italian, American Indian, Black, Armenian, Portuguese, Jewish, Syrian, and Chinese children.

We found that, while these traditions were being handed on among children in the short span of five or six years out of their lives (from five to eleven years of age), there was at the

same time a good deal of interplay among children of different ethnic backgrounds. We saw some Black children enthusiastically playing a game they had learned from a group of Chinese children nearby, but obviously quite unaware of the meaning of any of the oriental words they were chanting.

Children were friendly and eager to share their ordinary, everyday games once they saw our interest in learning from them. The sheer physical challenge of "Red Rover, Red Rover" was indeed a spectacular scrimmage to witness, and yet no one was hurt nor did it seem violent. Teasing rhymes ("Eddie Spaghetti"), expressing general disdain, had an impersonal air as though the children were being rude just for the fun of it. We watched these young children using the environment as their own domain for play—the pavements, walls of buildings, iron manhole covers, stoops, doorways, a mound of rubble, water hydrants, squares in the sidewalk, street gutters, lampposts.

We heard many examples of games that had topical references and additions from the children's television and pop song experience and from political influences as well. "Rinsle, Tinsle" must have evolved from a television commercial of the past; "The landlord rang my front door bell" is obviously borrowed from a current Chuck Berry pop song, and reference is also made to the Beatles' title "Yellow Submarine." "I'll be, be . . ." is taken from a Black Panther rally, and there are political twists on Mussolini, Kennedy, and Nixon. Sometimes old nursery tunes appear with contemporary words "Ringo, Ringo, Ringo Starr, how I wonder where you are?" Lines from the popular minstrel-show tune, "Ol' Dan Tucker" showed up again, passed on by oral tradition since the 1800s.

Jumping rope is one of the oldest games in the world and traditionally was done on Good Friday. In ancient times, when crops were planted in the spring, people would celebrate with jumping contests as well as with songs and dancing. It was believed that the crops would grow only as high as the people could jump, and possibly the game of jump rope had its origin in such rites. In the hop season in Europe, a hop stem, stripped of its

leaves, was used as rope for these games. In Greece they used vine strands for the same purpose. It was interesting for us to see the unique manner in which the Chinese children made *their* jump rope out of rubber bands. Thousands of children have taken up this particular form of rope jumping, and they all refer to it as "Chinese Jump Rope." We joined some Sioux Indian children skipping rope in a shaded corner of their school playground in Rapid City, South Dakota, and found them jumping to the same "Cinderella, dressed in yella . . ." which we heard in Boston the week before!

The Mohawk Indian child we found playing "Scully" with bottle caps in the streets of Brooklyn, New York, was a living part of the long tradition of marble-playing stemming from ancient history when the games were played with rough stones. We can still see the diagrams scratched out on the early Roman Forum pavements. (Today's "hopscotch"?)

In some agricultural societies, we still find ceremonies and incantations performed by adults to make rain, to fertilize the earth, to insure the success of the hunt, to frighten away evil spirits, and to celebrate the harvest. All our lives are touched with niceties that are ritualistic in some small form: blowing out the birthday candles, giving flowers to a loved one, cutting the wedding cake, carrying jack-o'-lanterns and bringing evergreens into the house at the winter solstice.

Crossing fingers, spitting, clenching fists ("bucking off"), accompanied by ancient ritual words, are an unself-conscious part of the ceremonial declarations of childhood. These activities are part of the unwritten culture of the world, having adult ritual and magical origins in many countries. Tug of war, or tugging on ropes, is found in the Far East as well as in Europe; blindman's buff was popular in medieval Europe, but it is part of a traditional masked ceremony found among some tribes of American Indians today. Can "London Bridge is falling down" be traced to adult rites for sacrificing a victim in the foundations of a new bridge so that his spirit could inhabit and protect it? Were victims for human sacrifice chosen by the same sort of chant that chil-

dren use to choose who shall be "It" for a game today? Are some of the nonsense rhymes remnants of spells and charms? Winding up around the tree ("Ring around a rosie") or bush ("Here we go round the mulberry bush"), and eventually the Maypole, was certainly a pre-Christian ceremony. Similarly, "Rattlesnake" is based on a ceremonial dance figure which eventually worked its way into country dancing and our square dance. Think of the various ways to insure safety or protection of the "hunted" from the "hunter" in the different games of tag! Children's pantomimes and performances can be traced back to primitive needs of identifying with the animal, plant, or hunt—acting out something you wish to be, or wish to happen, as a means of making it happen.

The functional work song sung by sailors, workers, convicts—and even mothers or fathers singing their children to sleep—is becoming less and less a part of our culture. But in the streets, children are still using tunes and chants to aid them in the rhythm of their complicated rope skipping and ball bouncing. Even the street cries of hawkers have disappeared, though remnants can occasionally be found in children's taunting and teasing chants based on the minor third interval. Hundreds of children's familiar songs feature this same interval, and these two notes are the basis for much of the liturgical chant in the church today.

As with all traditional folk material, there is a great deal of fluidity and mutation. Slight differences and changes are encountered in the same game or chant circulated by different children in different locations. There were moments when the children, who taught us these games, had to argue among themselves before they could agree on how a certain game went and what the rules were! So this collection is not in any way definitive, or to be followed rigidly for play or instruction. We have purposely made any bits of instruction sketchy to encourage improvisation, and we would recommend as little adult direction as possible in passing these games on to children. This collection gets increasingly freer and more imaginative in the later sections, and we hope this will encourage others to use this book as a starting point and go on to make up their *own* games.

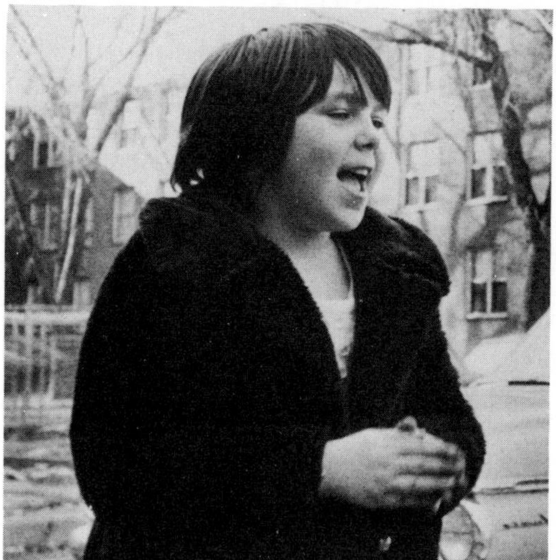

NAME CALLING

Eddie Spaghetti with the meatball eyes,
Put him in the oven and make french fries!

Sam, Sam, the dirty man,
Washed his face in a frying pan,
Combed his hair with the back of a chair,
And danced with a toothache in the air!

Míss Whíte hád a fríght
Ín the míddle óf the níght.
She sáw a ghóst éating toást
Hálfway úp the lámppóst.

Oh, you never went to college,
You never went to school,
But when it's time to boogie,
You can boogie like a fool!

RINGO, RINGO, RINGO STARR

Rin - go, Rin - go, Rin - go Starr, How I won - der
what you are. Un - der - neath that mop of hair,
Rin - go, are you real - ly there? Rin - go, Rin - go,
Rin - go Starr, How I won - der what you are.

Salami was a dancer,
She danced for the King,
And everytime she danced,
She wiggled every thing.
"Stop!" said the King,
"You can't do that here."
"Pooh!" said Salami,
And kicked him in the rear.

Sammy on the railway,
Picking up stones.
Along came an engine
And broke Sammy's nose.
"Oh," says Sammy,
"That's not fair."
"Oh," says the engine,
"I don't care!"

BALL BOUNCING

Héllo, héllo, Bíll.
Whére are you goíng, Bíll?
Uṕtoẃn, Bíll.
Whát fór, Bíll?
To páy the gás bíll.
Hów múch, Bíll?
A tén dóllar bíll.

Cóncentrátion the létter *Á*
May Í repéat the létter *Á*
Becaúse I liḱe the létter *Á*
Ápple begíns with the létter *Á*.

Concentration the letter *B*
May I repeat the letter *B*
Because I like the letter *B*
Ball begins with the letter *B*.

C — Cat
D — Dog
E — Eagle
F — Fan

G — Glenny
H — Hot Dog
I — Indians
J — Jack, etc.

DOWN BY THE RIVER

Down by the riv - ver where the green grass grows,
Where lit - tle Ma - ry wa - shes her clothes, She sang, she
sang, she sang so sweet, that she sang Pa - trick a -
cross the street. Ma - ry made a dump - ling, she
made it so sweet. She cut it up in sli - ces and
gave us all a piece, saying: "Take this, take this, and
don't be slow, For to - mor - row is my wed - ding day and
I must go!"

Down in the valley where the green grass grows,
There sits Kennedy as sweet as a rose.
Along came Nixon and kissed him on the cheek.
How many kisses did he receive?
1 2 3 4 5 6 etc.

THE WONDER BALL

The ball is passed round the circle. Each time, the one holding the ball on the last word, "found," is eliminated; until only one remains.

The won-der ball goes round and round, If you're the
one___ you are bound. Pass it quick - ly, you are
bound, If you're the one___ you are found.

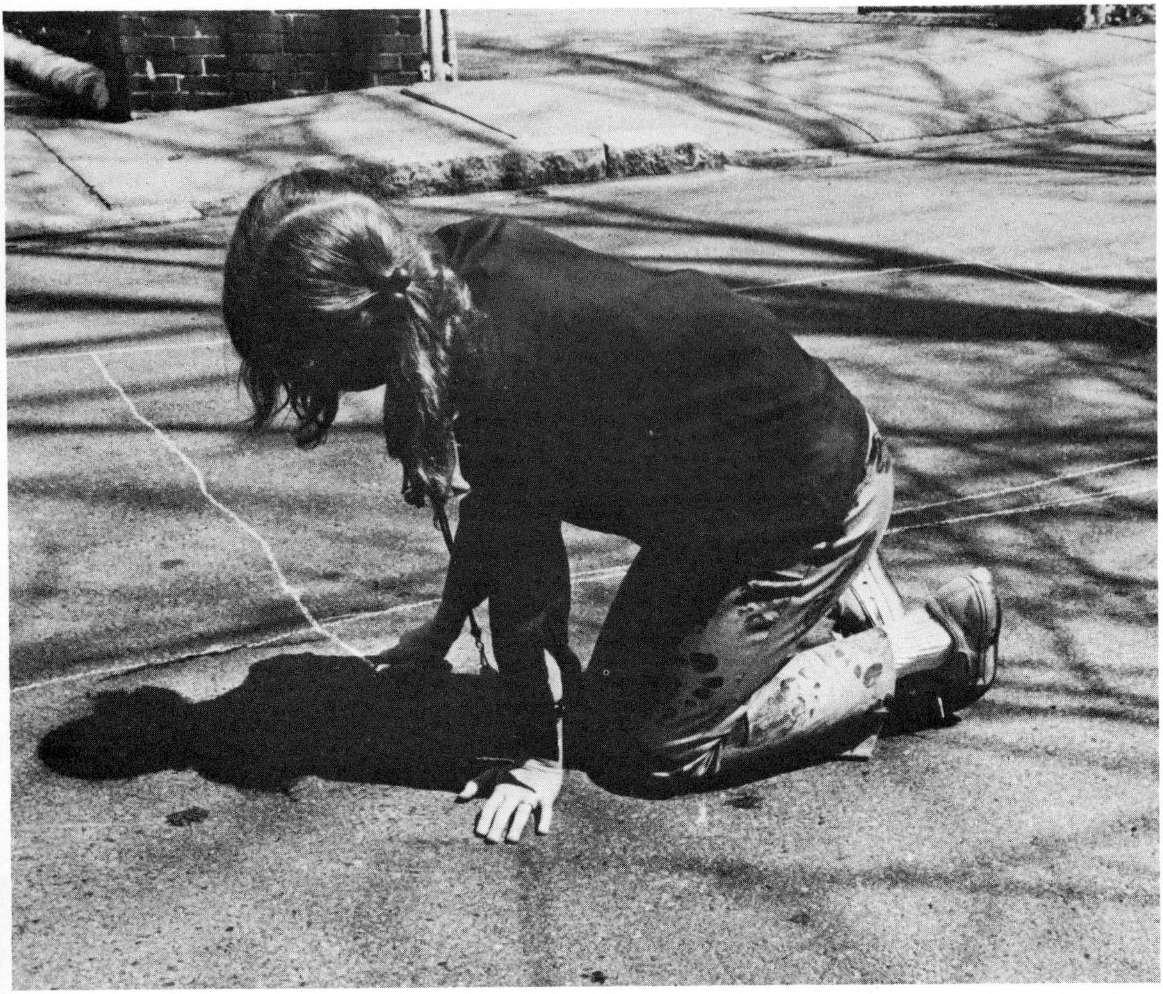

SIDEWALK DRAWING GAMES

4 SQUARE

This game is played with four people, each standing in one of four numbered squares. A ball is thrown and caught by the players: player 1 to 2, 2 to 3, 3 to 4, and 4 can throw it to anyone. If a player misses a catch, he's out and goes to the end of a waiting line of players. Then the one who threw the ball moves into the empty square; everyone else moves up a square, if possible, and the first person in line moves into square 1.

Player 4 remains in his square until he misses a catch and then he is out. The center circle (B) is a safe zone; if the ball lands there, no player is out.

The main object of the game is to arrive at square 4 and keep it.

STANLEY CUP
CHAMPS

SCULLY

is played with bottle caps. Each player shoots his bottle cap at the number in order, starting with 1. If the cap lands on the right number, he gets another turn. If he aims at and hits another player's cap, he can proceed directly to his number. After reaching 13, he goes backward down to 1; then wins by hitting his opponent's cap five times.

3
5
7
2
12
13
9
10
11
1
8
6
4

CIRCLE GAMES

LITTLE SALLY WATER

Lit - tle Sal - ly Wat - er sit - ting in a sau - cer,

Cry - ing and weep - ing for some - one to come.

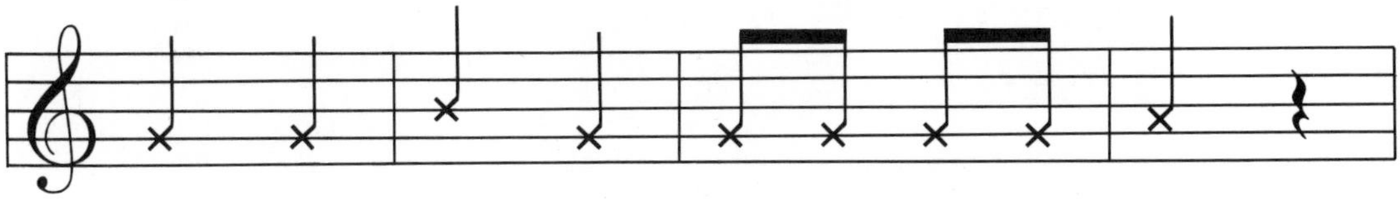

Rise up, Sal - ly, Wipe a - way your tears.

Turn to the East, Sal - ly, turn to the West,

Turn to the one that you love best.

Sally sits
in the middle.
She rises up,
turns around, and
chooses someone—
the next Sally.

BLUE BIRD

Everyone makes a circle, holding hands. One person weaves in and out under the raised arms. During the second verse, he stands behind someone and taps him on the shoulder. Then the weaving starts over with the new person following behind the weaver. By the end, everyone has joined the weaving.

Blue bird, Blue bird through my win - dow, Blue bird, Blue bird
through my win - dow, Blue bird, Blue bird through my win - dow.
Oh! John - ny, I'm___ tir - ed. Take a lit - tle girl,
tap her on the shoul - der, Take a lit - tle girl,
tap her on the shoul - der, Take a lit - tle girl,
tap her on the shoul - der. Oh! John - ny, I'm___ tir - ed.

I WAS RIDING THROUGH THE COUNTRY

I was rid - ing through the coun - try, I was
rid - ing through the field, And I met a señ - o -
ri - ta with the buck - les on her heel. Oh,
(QUICKLY)
sha - kee, sha - kee, sha - kee, Shake it once a - gain.
Round and round and round she goes,
where she stops no - bo - dy knows.

GLORY TO THE MOUNTAIN

A circle is made holding hands and singing, while moving in a clockwise direction. A leader is outside the circle going around in the opposite direction. When the song says, "one, two, three . . ." the leader taps three people, who leave the center circle and follow him in the outside circle.

When one person is left in the center, the others all stop moving and face into the middle bowing to the *Mountain,* as they sing the end part of the song. The *Mountain* becomes the new leader.

(WALKING TEMPO)
Oh, we'll all sing glo - ry to the moun - tain. The
moun - tain is so high, It reach - es to the sky.
(ALL BUT LAST TIME)
And it's one two three fol - low me,
(LAST TIME)
and we'll And we'll all ____ bow ____ to the moun -tain.

DUCK, DUCK, GOOSE

Played sitting in a circle with legs crossed. The child who is *It* goes around tapping each head saying, "Duck, duck, duck, duck, duck . . . Goose!"—landing on someone. The *Goose* then chases *It* who tries to return to the empty place before he's caught.

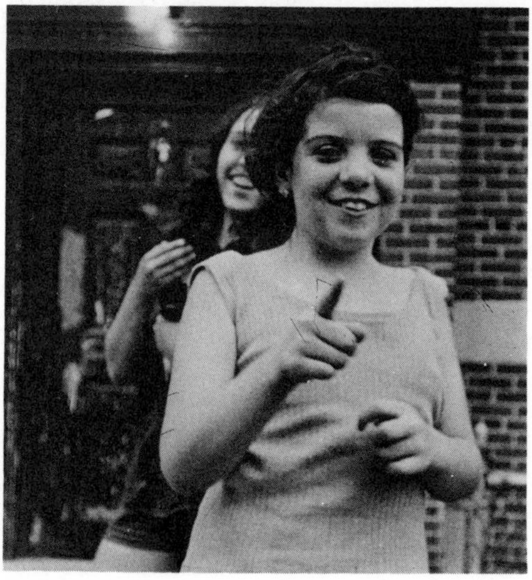

WHO'S It?

ICKABOCKER BOO

My mother and your mother
Live across the way.
Everytime they have a fight,
This is what they say:
    Ickabocker, ickabocker, ickabocker boo!
    Ickabocker, soda cracker, out goes *you!*

Engine, engine, number nine
Going down Chicago line.
If the train goes off the track,
You're the one to bring it back.
    Yes, No, Yes, No.
    The sky is blue. How old are you?
    "10"
    1 2 3 4 5 6 7 8 9 10!

(The person you end on is *It.*)

BUCKING OFF

Choose; "Odds" "Evens"

1-2-3 shoot! (odds)
1-2-3 shoot! (evens)
1-2-3 shoot! (evens)

(Evens wins)

Two kids choose odds or evens. On the word "shoot" they throw out a certain number of fingers, calling which way the count fell. The winner gets first choice of pickings for his team.

TAG GAMES

TIVVY TAG

When you squat, you're safe if you say;

"Tivvy Tag"
or "Bat Man"
or "Bunny Rabbit"—then you can't be tagged.

RED ROVER

Two teams line up facing each other:

"Red Rover, Red Rover, send *Joey* right over!"

Joey runs as fast as he can and tries to break through the line of linked hands—if successful, he joins them on their team.

STEAL THE BACON

The players form two equal teams (plus a *number caller*) on either side of a can. Players on each team are numbered, so that there are opposing number *ones, twos,* etc. When the players' numbers are called, they rush out and try to grab the can back behind their own team line, without getting tagged. If the *number caller* shouts the word "bacon," everyone can try to grab the can.

Examples said by the Number Caller:

"*One* thing happened *to* me."
"That team over there isn't *too* smart."
"Three."
"I had orange juice and toast and oatmeal and pizza
and a little piece of *bacon* on the side."

"There is *one too* many people over there."
"I found four balls this morning; *one* more *too*."
"Where did those *three* shoes go?"
"This morning my mother cooked me some awful cereal,
two eggs, and some icky *bacon*."

JUMP ROPE

Jelly in the dish
Makes me sick.
A wiggle and a woggle,
And a two forty six.
Not because you're dirty, not because you're clean;
It's just because you kissed a boy
Behind a magazine.
How many kisses do you want?
"5" 1 2 3 4 5

Éskimo, Éskimo, Éskimo Píe.
Túrn aroúnd and toúch the sḱy.

Únder . . .
(*You slip under the rope to the other side.*)
Óver . . .
(*One jump in and then out to the original side.*)
Únder and over the móon,
My fáther lost his hát.
Picḱed it up and pút it on,
Nów it's time for béd,
For béd,
For béd.

Rinsle, Tinsle
The ordinary soap.
Judy is a dope,
A dope, a dope.

TEDDY BEAR

I had a little teddy bear, his name was Tiny Tim.
I put him in the bathtub to see if he could swim.
He drank all the water, he ate all the soap,
He died the next morning with a bubble in his throat.
In came the doctor, in came the nurse,
In came the lady with the alligator purse.
"Penicillin," said the doctor. "Penicillin," said the nurse.
"Penicillin," said the lady with the alligator purse.
Out walked the doctor, out walked the nurse,
Out walked the lady with the alligator purse.

CHINESE JUMP ROPE

Played with a chain of rubber bands. The jump rope is stretched between two people and kept low to the ground. Various jumps and tricks are done while the rope is raised higher and higher until all players are caught out, and the highest jumper wins.

Í can do the crísscross.
Í can do the kíck.
Í can do the óverall,
And álso the splít.

LANDLORD

My land - lord ring my front door bell (a ding -
dong). Let it ring for a long, long time.
Peek through the win - dows, Peek through the blinds,
Ask that man what was on his mind. Said - a
mon - ey, hon - ey, 1 2 Said - a mon - ey, hon - ey.
3 4 Said - a mon - ey, hon - ey.

etc. 5 - 6, 7 - 8, 9 - 10
until jumper trips!

Girl Scout, Girl Scout, dressed in blue,
These are the motions you must do:
Stand at attention, stand at ease,
Bend your elbows, bend your knees.
Salute to the Captain, bow to the Queen,
Turn your back on the yellow submarine.
I can do the heel-toe, I can do the splits.
I can do the wiggle-waggle just like this!

I'ĺl be, bé,
Wal̗king down the streét,
Tén times a weék.
Un-gáwa, un-gáwa, (baby)
This is my power.
Whát is the stóry?
Whát is the stríke?
I sáid it, I meánt it.
I réally répresent it.
Take a cóol, cool Bláck to knóck me dówn.
Take a cóol, cool Bláck to knóck me óut.
I'm sweét, I'm kínd,
I'm sóul sister númber nine.
Don't líke my aṕples,
Don't sháke my treé,
I'm a Cástle Square Bláck,
Don't meśs with ḿe.

UP AND DOWN JAMAICA PLAIN

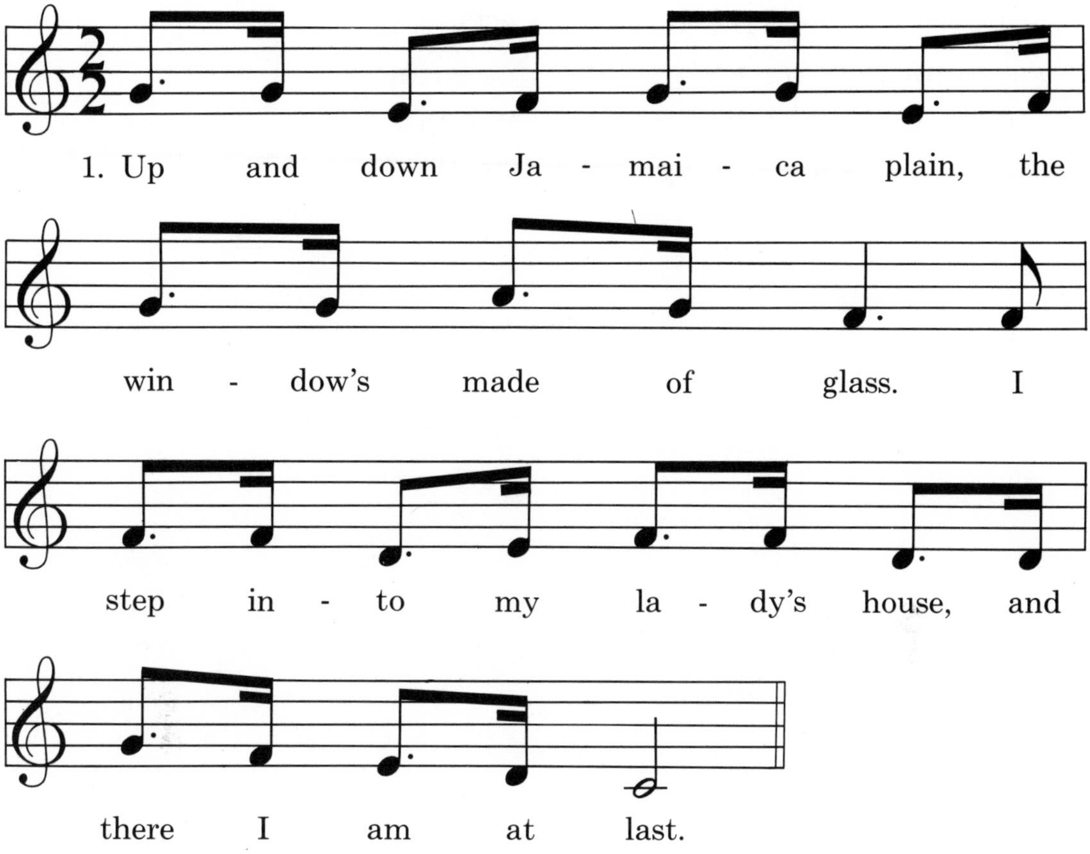
1. Up and down Ja - mai - ca plain, the
win - dow's made of glass. I
step in - to my la - dy's house, and
there I am at last.

2. My first name is *Dorothy,*
Catch me if you can.
She's in love with *Paul,*
And he's the greatest man.

3. I took her out in the garden.
I sat her on my knee.
I asked my darling *Dorothy,*
If she would marry me.

Yes. No. Maybe so.
Yes. No. Maybe so. . . .

ANGELS, DEVILS

One person stands circling a jump rope out flat on the ground. All stand around while one jumps over it and says, "Angels, Devils, Angels, Devils," etc. Whichever word you miss on, you are!

PAUL
JERRY

ACTION GAMES

R — A — T —
T — L — E — —
S — N — A — K — E spells
Rattlesnake!

This is repeated over and over while the line winds up their arms. When all have gone under, they form a tight backward circle and jump up and down yelling one more verse at the top of their lungs.

KING OF THE CASTLE

Í'm on the Kíng's land,
The Kíng's not at hóme.
The Kíng's gone to Bóston
To búy his wife a cómb.

SEVEN UP

Seven kids are *It.* (You can use fewer if you don't have a very large group.) The rest of the group sits with their heads down and eyes shut tight. Each of the seven goes and taps one person on the head. Each tapped person raises his hand, not peeking. After seven hands are up, everyone can look, and the seven tapped try to guess who just tapped them. Whoever guesses right gets to be a tapper.

LONDON BRIDGE

1. London Bridge is falling down,
   Falling down, falling down,
   London Bridge is falling down,
   My fair lady.

LeSabre

2. Take the key and lock her up,
Lock her up, lock her up,
Take the key and lock her up,
My fair lady.

FOLLOW THE LEADER

LEAP FROG

HULA HOOP

TELEPHONE

Everyone sits in a circle. One person begins by whispering a "secret" to the person next to him, then each person passes it on in a whisper. The last person says it out loud, and the changes from the original can be very funny!

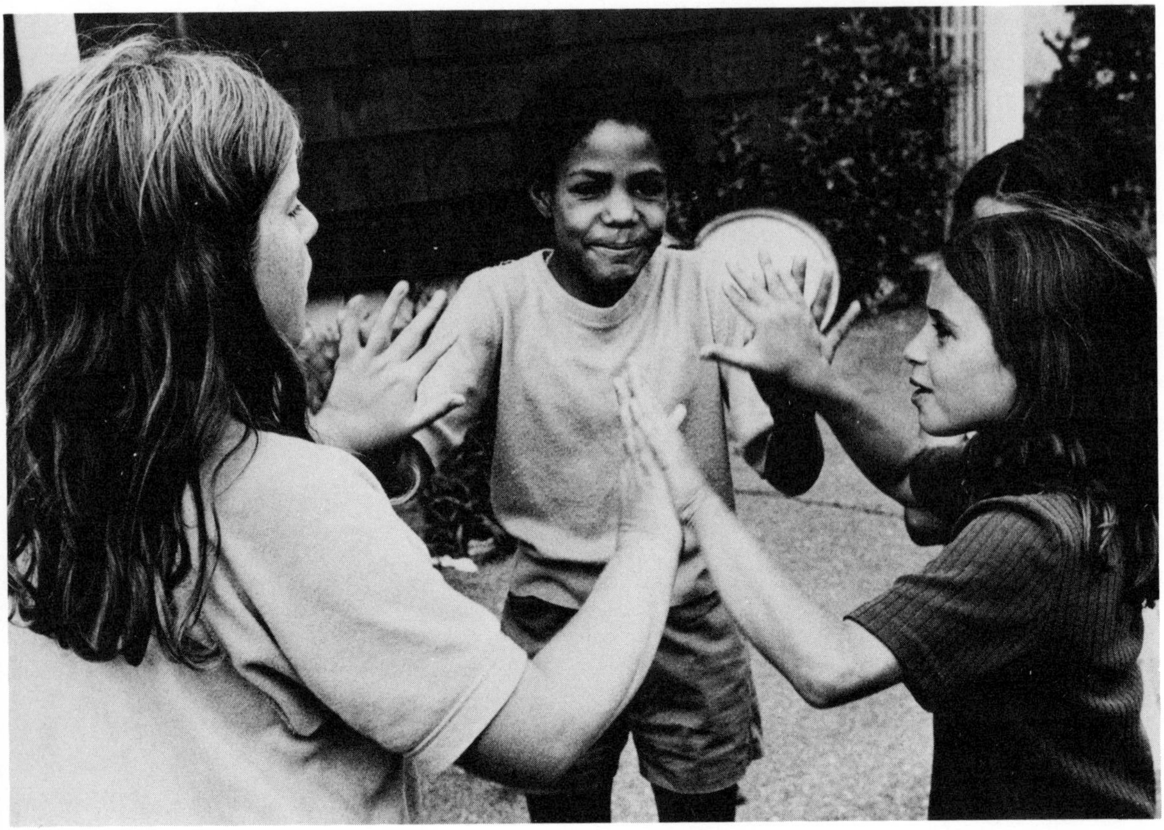

HAND CLAPPING

HAVE YOU EVER, EVER, EVER

1. Have you ever, ever, ever,
   In a long-legged life,
   Seen a long-legged sailor
   With a long-legged wife?

   No I never, never, never,
   In a long-legged life,
   Saw a long-legged sailor
   With a long-legged wife.

2. Have you ever, ever, ever,
   In a pigeon-toed life,
   Seen a pigeon-toed sailor
   With a pigeon-toed wife?

   No, I . . .

3. Have you ever, ever, ever,
   In a Chinese life . . .

4. Have you ever, ever, ever,
   In a short-legged life . . .

With each type there belongs a gesture which describes the characters.

SHIMMY, SHIMMY, COKE-CA-POP!

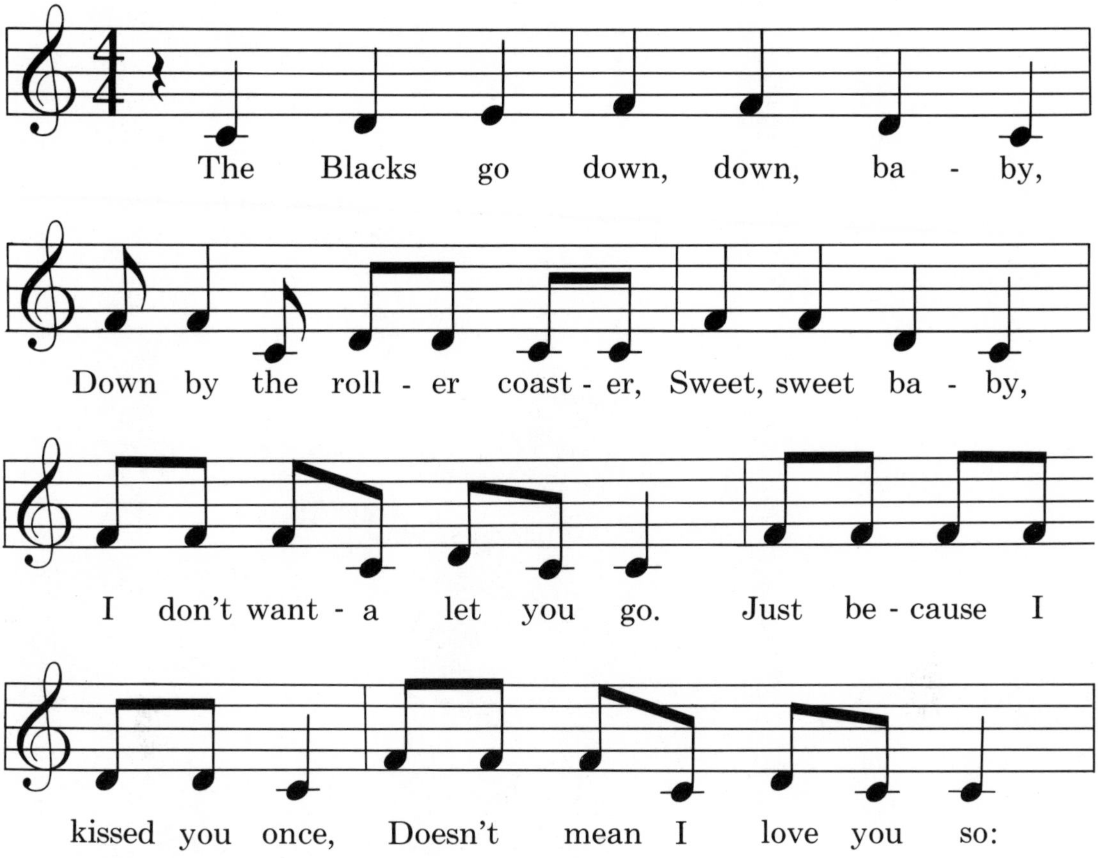
The Blacks go down, down, ba - by,
Down by the roll - er coast - er, Sweet, sweet ba - by,
I don't want - a let you go. Just be - cause I
kissed you once, Doesn't mean I love you so:

(CHANTED)

Shimmy, shimmy, shimmy, shimmy,
Shimmy, shimmy, pop!
Shimmy, shimmy, shimmy, shimmy,
Shimmy, shimmy, coke-ca-pop!

OLD LADY MAC

Old La - dy Mac, Mac, Mac, All dressed in
black, black, black, With sil - ver buttons, buttons buttons,
All down her back, back, back. She can - not . . .

. . . read, read, read.
She cannot write, write, write,
But she can smoke, smoke, smoke
Her father's pipe, pipe, pipe.
She asked her mother, mother, mother
For fifty cents, cents, cents
To see the elephant, elephant, elephant
Jump over the fence, fence, fence.
He jumped so high, high, high,
He reached the sky, sky, sky,
And he never came back, back, back
Till the Fourth of July, July, July;
And that's a lie, lie, lie
The doctor said, said, said
She bumped her head, head, head
On a piece of corn bread, bread, bread.
The doctor went, went, went
To make his bed, bed, bed;
He bumped his head, head, head
On a piece of corn bread, bread, bread.
He went to Par, Par, Par
To buy a car, car, car,
And that's the end, end, end
Of Lady Mac, Mac, Mac.

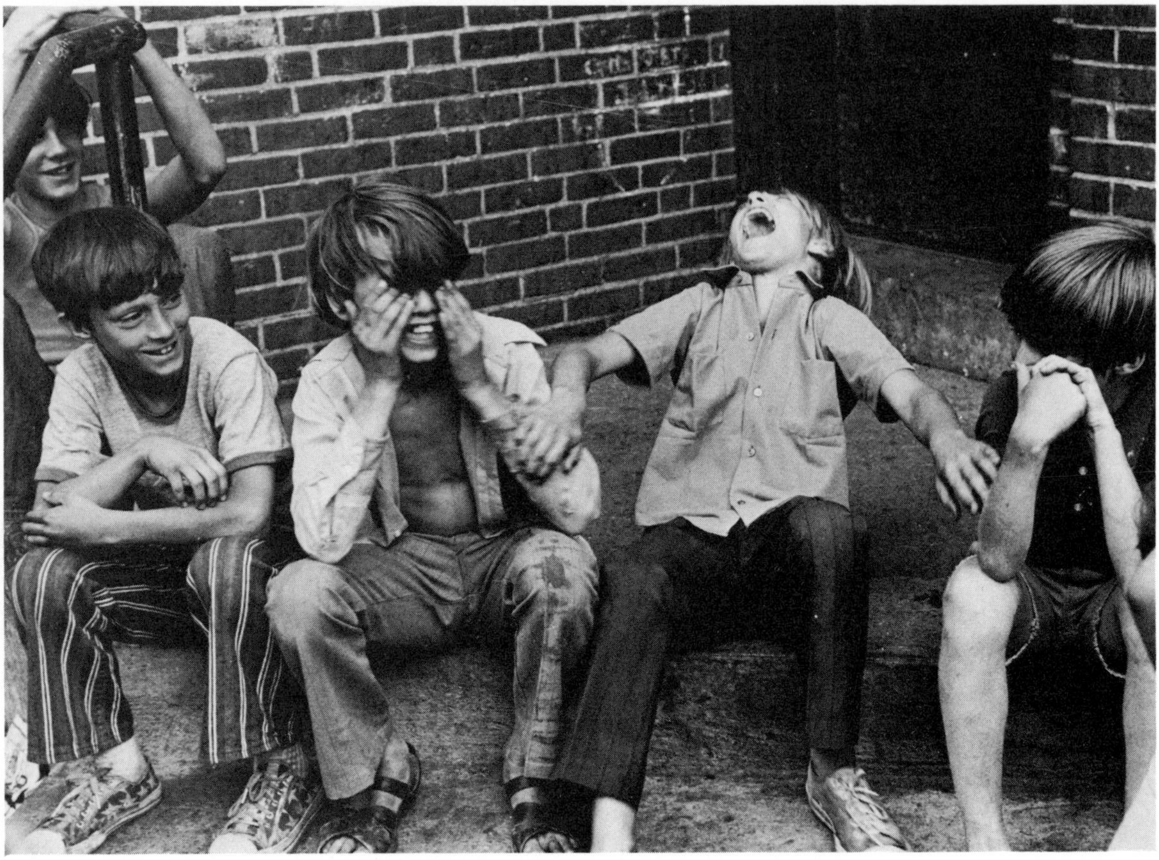

DRAMATIC PLAY

THE WITCH GAME

THE GROUP: Hey, old witch, are you coming out tonight?
WITCH: No!
THE GROUP: Why?
WITCH: I'm taking a bath.

(or) I'm putting on my bra.
I have to cook my dinner.
I have to haunt my teddy bear.
I'm haunting the house on the hill.
My black cat is sick.
etc.

The group asks the two questions as they move toward the witch. She makes up scary witchlike answers until the group is close. Then she suddenly yells Yes! instead of No, and tries to catch someone as he's running away. The one she catches is the new witch.

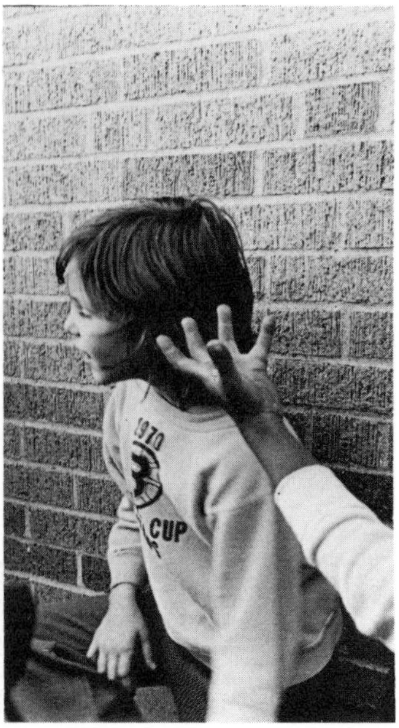
1970
CUP

CHINESE SQUARE

This game takes place on a sidewalk square in the pavement. Five kids play, with one on each corner of the square and *It* in the middle. *It* calls out the titles in the game and can make up new ones.

LAUNDRY

The corners stretch out their arms and become clotheslines. *It* checks to see if the laundry is dry. The corners slap their arms down fast and try to catch *It*.

LETTER

It draws a circle on each corner's back. The corner has to guess the letter within the circle.

MONKEY CLIMBS THE TREE
It tickles up a corner's leg trying to make her laugh.

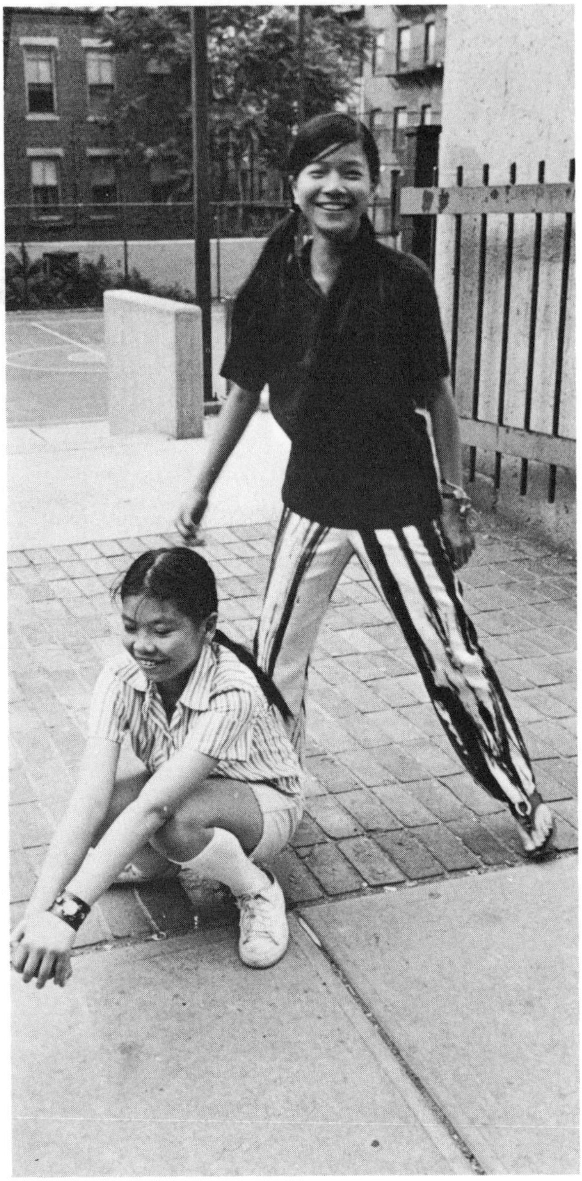

STORY TIME

It announces "Story Time." The others reply: "How many letters?" *It* gives a number: "10." All walk ten steps then run back. Last one back is *It*.

PICKING UP A ROCK

Corners all crouch down and make shapes like rocks. *It* tries to pick each one up. Whoever can be picked up becomes *It*.

DIXIE GIRLS

All
①
We are lit - tle Dix - ie girls stand - ing in a row. I'm
② ③ All
Sam, I'm Sammy, I'm Sam. We are lit - tle Dix - ie girls
① ② ③
twirl - ing in a row, Twirl - ing in a row, Twirl - ing in a row.
① ② ③
S - A - M, S - A - M - M - Y, S - A - M,
①
We are lit - tle Dix - ie girls twirl - ing in a row. I'm
② ③
1 I'm 2, I'm 3, I'm ① I got a boy friend that you
4 5 6 ②
7 8 9 ③
can't beat. ① Mine is tall with dark black hair that you can't beat. etc.
② brown
③ red

A song-dance made up by three girls. They invented their own tune and words and also danced and acted it out in a taunting, boasting manner.

We are little Dixie girls twirling in a row,
    Twirling in a row, twirling in a row.
    I'm 1, I'm 2, I'm 3,
    I'm 4, I'm 5, I'm 6,
    I'm 7, I'm 8, I'm 9.
We are little Dixie girls standing in a row.
    I got a boy friend that you can't beat.
    I got a boy friend that you can't beat.
    I got a boy friend that you can't beat.
    Mine is tall with dark black hair that you can't beat.
    Mine is tall with dark brown hair that you can't beat.
    Mine is tall with dark red hair that you can't beat, etc.
We are little Dixie girls standing in a row.

    clap (turn right)

We are little Dixie girls standing in a row.

    clap (turn left)

We are little Dixie girls walking in a row.
We are little Dixie girls bowing in a row.

(On the word "bowing," they all fall down.)

Here's a song for kite flying!

Three lit - tle an - gels all dressed in white,
Trying to get to hea - ven on the end of a kite. The
kite string broke and down they all fell. In -
stead of going to hea - ven, They all went to . . .
(ENDING)
Two lit - tle an - gels . . . all went to *zero!*

Two little angels all dressed in white,
Trying to get to heaven on the end of a kite.
The kite string broke and down they all fell,
Instead of going to heaven they all went to . . .

One little angel . . .

Three little devils all dressed in red,
Trying to get to heaven on the end of a thread.
But the thread string broke and down they all fell,
Instead of going to heaven they all went to . . .

Two little devils . . .
One little devil . . .

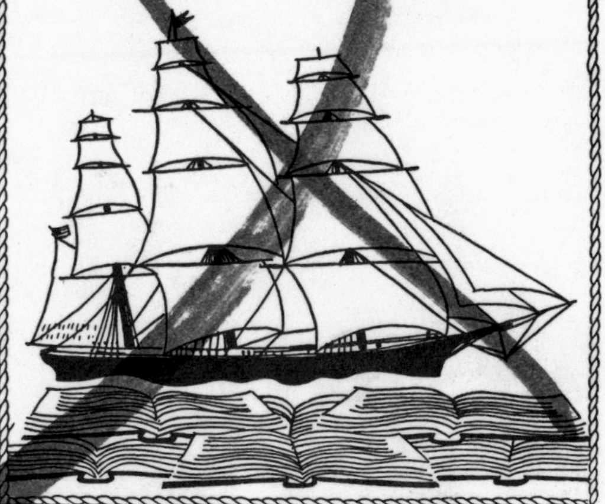

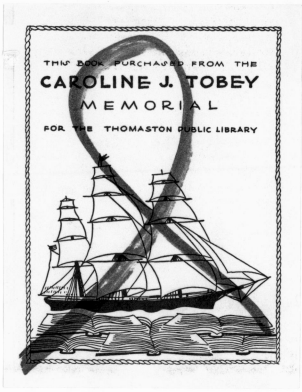